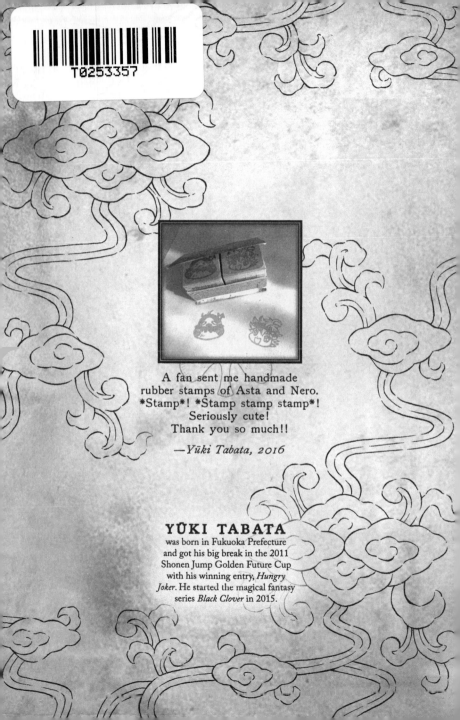

A fan sent me handmade
rubber stamps of Asta and Nero.
Stamp! *Stamp stamp stamp*!
Seriously cute!
Thank you so much!!

—*Yūki Tabata, 2016*

YŪKI TABATA
was born in Fukuoka Prefecture
and got his big break in the 2011
Shonen Jump Golden Future Cup
with his winning entry, *Hungry
Joker*. He started the magical fantasy
series *Black Clover* in 2015.

BLACK CLOVER
VOLUME 5
SHONEN JUMP Manga Edition

Story and Art by YŪKI·TABATA

Translation ✦ TAYLOR ENGEL,
HC LANGUAGE SOLUTIONS, INC.

Touch-Up Art & Lettering ✦ ANNALIESE CHRISTMAN

Design ✦ FAWN LAU

Editor ✦ ALEXIS KIRSCH

Printed in the U.S.A.

Published by VIZ Media, LLC
P.O. Box 77010
San Francisco, CA 94107

10 9 8 7 6 5
First printing, February 2017
Fifth printing, April 2022

viz.com

Klaus

Gauche

Charmy

Mimosa

Asta

Black✦Clover

YŪKI TABATA　5　LIGHT

Yuno

Squad: The Golden Dawn
Magic: Wind

Asta's best friend, and a good rival who's been working to become the Wizard King right alongside him since they were little.

Asta

Squad: The Black Bulls
Magic: None (Anti-Magic)

He has no magic, but he's working to become the Wizard King through sheer guts and his well-trained body.

Charmy Pappitson

Squad: The Black Bulls
Magic: Cotton

She's small, but she eats like a maniac.

Noelle Silva

Squad: The Black Bulls
Magic: Water

A royal. She's really impudent, but can be kind too.

Finral Roulacase

Squad: The Black Bulls
Magic: Spatial

A flirt who likes girls so much it gets in the way of his missions.

Luck Voltia

Squad: The Black Bulls
Magic: Lightning

A battle maniac who smiles constantly and has a problematic personality.

Nero

A mysterious bird that always follows Asta around for some reason.

Gauche Adlai

Squad: The Black Bulls
Magic: Mirror

A former convict with a blind, pathological love for his little sister.

Fuegoleon Vermillion

Squad: The Crimson Lion Kings
Magic: Flame

A captain with a strong sense of justice. He's Mimosa's cousin and Leopold's older brother.

Julius Novachrono

Wizard King

The strongest mage in the Clover Kingdom. Also a peerless magic fanatic.

Rades

Squad: The Eye of the Midnight Sun
Magic: Wraith

He once belonged to a Magic Knights brigade, but was exiled.

Mimosa Vermillion

Squad: The Golden Dawn
Magic: Plant

Noelle's cousin. She's calm, gentle, and a bit of an airhead.

❋   ❋   ❋

STORY

In a world where magic is everything, Asta and Yuno are both found abandoned on the same day at a church in the remote village of Hage. Both dream of becoming the Wizard King, the highest of all mages, and they spend their days working toward that dream.

The year they turn 15, both receive grimoires, magic books that amplify their bearer's magic. They take the entrance exam for the Magic Knights, nine groups of mages under the direct control of the Wizard King. Yuno, whose magic is strong, joins the Golden Dawn, an elite group, while Asta, who has no magic at all, joins the Black Bulls, a group of misfits. With this, the two finally take their first step toward becoming the Wizard King…

The Magic Knights engage in a fierce battle against the terrorist group that launched a surprise attack on the royal capital. However, the results are brutal: Fuegoleon sustains massive injuries that leave him near death, and Asta is abducted. Calling themselves The Eye of the Midnight Sun, the enemies claim they will destroy the kingdom, then they vanish…

BLACK ❋ CLOVER

CONTENTS

BLACK ✿ CLOVER

5

WE HAVE TO SAVE HIM!!

ASTA...

THEY TOOK ASTA!

NO.

YES, BUT...!

NOELLE...!

WE CAN'T. I'M SORRY, BUT THERE'S NO WAY TO LOCATE THEIR DESTINATION!

...

WE DON'T HAVE THE TIME OR THE MAGIC TO SPEND ON SOMEONE LIKE HIM.

RIGHT NOW, OUR TOP PRIORITY IS REINFORCING THE CAPITAL'S DEFENSES. THERE'S NO GUARANTEE THAT THOSE WERE THE ONLY ENEMIES.

SHUF

HELP CAPTAIN FUEGO-LEON!!

MIMOSA!!

HA

!

ENDED UP LIKE THIS...?!

THIS CAN'T BE... SOMEONE LIKE FUEGOLEON...

...

OH... ASTA ...!

PLEASE, PLEASE BE ALL RIGHT!!

FLAAA

LEOPOLD TOO...!

FLAAA

WHAT COULD HAVE DONE THIS TO A MAGIC KNIGHT CAPTAIN?!

MUTTER MUTTER

HE NEEDS TO BE TAKEN TO THE MEDICAL WARD FOR MORE ADVANCED HEALING MAGIC, OR...OR ELSE...!

WITH MY MAGIC, FIRST AID IS THE BEST I CAN DO!

FLAAA

PFT!

SOLID...! HOW COULD YOU SAY THAT?!

THE VERMILLION CLAN SURE AIN'T WHAT IT USED TO BE. MAKES ME EMBARRASSED TO BE A ROYAL...!

SOME CAPTAIN. THAT'S JUST PATHETIC!

UNLESS WE WIN, OUR EXISTENCE IS POINTLESS.

SHUF

WE ARE MAGIC KNIGHTS!

HOWEVER, SOLID...

HE'S RIGHT!! THIS IS GONNA TRASH THE REPUTATION OF THE CRIMSON LION KINGS TOO!

...

NOZEL ...!

10

AS WE WERE NOT EVEN PRESENT AT THE FIGHT, WE ARE LESS THAN HE IS.

STRENGTHEN THE DEFENSES SO THAT THE DAMAGE SPREADS NO FARTHER!

...

UH, RIGHT ...!

...

THANKS TO THAT, REINFORCEMENTS FROM OUTSIDE THE NOBLE REALM FAILED TO ARRIVE!

WE CAN'T LET OUR GUARD DOWN YET!!

HE'S RIGHT!! THEY SPREAD AROUND MAGIC THAT BLOCKS TRANSMISSION SPELLS, AND THE CHAIN OF COMMAND IS IN CHAOS!!

ASTA
....!

SHUF

SIMPLY ACHIEVING THE OBJECTIVE WOULDN'T HAVE TAKEN HALF THIS MUCH WORK!

"I WANT TO FIGHT A CAPTAIN ALONE!" YOU SAID. "I WANT TO LAY WASTE TO THE CAPITAL!" CONCEITED FOOL!

RADES! WE ENDED UP WITH A HUGE HEADACHE BECAUSE YOU STEPPED OUT OF LINE!

That's no skin off your noses!!

Shaddup!!

My toys are what took damage!!

DON'T GET CARRIED AWAY JUST BECAUSE THE MASTER HAS TAKEN A LIKING TO YOU.

We got what we went in for, so it's all good!

Like I care about that hag!!

Hag...

Buuut... it sounds like Catherine was defeated and is still out cold in the capital.

Ungh...

Huh?! No way! You know he's anti-magic, right?! This is on a different level than a mere magic-weakening effect!

I am going to use him in my research!

By the way, Sally.

We can't take that boy with us. Kill him.

Oh crap!! Did... did I get caught by the enemy?!

Ah!

Huh?!

Yeah! Let me kill him! I'm gonna make him into a toy!

Rades, you be quiet!

Only those acknowledged by our master can go there.

Don't cause unneeded trouble. Kill him before the meeting time.

Where... am I...?

What is this...??

It feels kinda nice...

YOU ASK THEM TOO!

FWSH

YOU'RE AWAKE!

A...A LADY?!

This lady's bad news!

Right, right, right??

You want me to investigate every last inch of you and your grimoire and run all sorts of experiments on you, right? You want to be useful to my research, right??

GIVE 'IM TO ME!!

TAKK

C'MON, PLEASE? I'LL ASK TOO, SO C'MON! PLEEEEEASE?!

WHATEVER HAPPENS, DON'T COME CRYING TO ME.

Sigh...

TAKK

And this is a really, really nasty situation!

BUT...
BUT
THAT'S...

...

WHA
...!!

HUH?

THE WIZARD KING... JULIUS NOVACHRONO?!!

HOW WAS THE CAPITAL?

D·I·E...

FWD

...

WHY IS THIS MAN HERE?!!

WHY HERE?!!

IT WOULD HAVE BEEN A BIT TOO HARD WITH NUMBERS LIKE THESE...

I KILLED THEM.

RESTRAINING YOU, I MEAN.

WHAT ...?!!

I... IMPOS- SIBLE!!

RRGH...

HUH ?!

HUH ?!

WAAAUGH!

WA!

BOOM

YOU CAN'T POSSIBLY HAVE GONE TO KILL...

...WITHOUT BEING PREPARED TO *BE* KILLED. RIGHT?

YOU JUST CAME FROM ATTACKING THE CAPITAL, DIDN'T YOU?

20

YOU SEEM PRETTY SKILLED. I'LL PROBABLY HAVE TROUBLE HERE.

THAT SAID...

WHAT POWER... SO THIS IS...THE WIZARD KING!!

...

THIS IS BAD... MY MAGIC IS ALREADY DRAINED!

IT'S FIRST COME, FIRST SERVED.

WHAT DO YOU THINK?

WHAT DO YOU SAY? I'LL LET JUST ONE OF YOU LIVE. WANT TO SURRENDER?

DON'T SELL US SHORT!!!

MY EYES CAN'T EVEN FOLLOW HIM!!

I GUESS THERE'S NO HELP FOR IT.

...

WHA... HOW IS HE MOVING LIKE THAT...?!

I MIGHT BE ABLE TO HANDLE NUMBERS LIKE THESE.

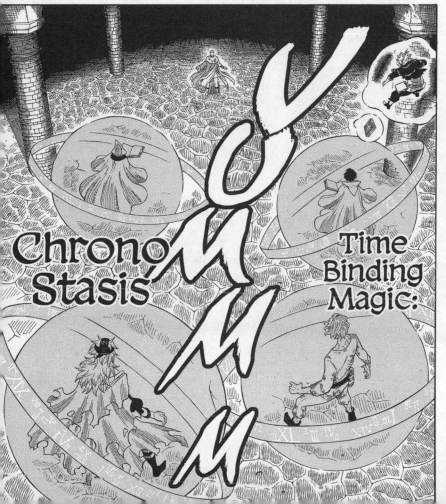

Time Binding Magic: Chrono Stasis

I CAN'T... MOVE...

WHAT... THE... HECK... IS... THIS...?!

...

SEE HOW IT FEELS TO LIVE...

...IN ONE UNENDING MOMENT.

NICE, I GOT ALL OF YOU.

WERE YOU MORE WORN OUT THAN I THOUGHT?

OH!

HELLO, ASTA.

WE SEEM TO BE LINKED BY FATE SOMEHOW.

SPLAT

DWAH!

THIS IS...

THOSE GUYS WERE REALLY TOUGH... AND HE GOT ALL OF THEM, JUST LIKE THAT!!

THIS IS... THE POWER OF THE WIZARD KING!!

IN THAT CASE, DON'T LOOK AWAY. WATCH CAREFULLY.

THIS IS WHAT YOU'RE AIMING FOR, ISN'T IT? TO BECOME WIZARD KING.

...MY GOAL! THE STRONGEST GUY!!

THIS IS ONLY A SMALL FRACTION OF WHAT YOU'LL HAVE TO SURPASS.

Julius
Novachrono

Age: 42
Height: 180 cm
Birthday: October 15
Sign: Libra
Blood Type: AB
Likes: Transforming and
       wandering around in
       search of new spells.

THE STRONGEST MAGE IN THE KINGDOM! THE ONE I NEED TO SURPASS!!

THIS IS THE WIZARD KING!!

CAN YOU STAND?

YOU CAN'T LOSE HERE!!

...

RRGH RRGH

... AFTER SEEING HIS POWER... I CAN'T STOP SHAKING!

WHOA...

BRR BRR

BAM

YOU IDIOT!!

Y...

SMIRK

I GUESS... YOU DIDN'T NEED HELP?

WEEZ WEEZ

...

SHUF

NOW, THEN...

THERE ARE SOME THINGS I WANT TO ASK YOU.

TAK TAK

YOU FOUR HAD SOME PRETTY INTERESTING MAGIC.

I WAS SURPRISED.

SHUF

WHAT ARE THESE JEWELS AND THIS STONE SLAB, HM...?

I'VE NEVER SEEN THE CHARACTERS OR THE PATTERN BEFORE.

WHAT WERE YOU TRYING TO DO WITH IT?

...

WE'LL HAVE THIS TALK LATER, AT LEISURE, IN THE CLOVER KINGDOM.

WELL, EVEN IF I ASK NOW, YOU CAN'T DO A THING INSIDE THAT SPELL.

...

TAK TAK

SOMETHING'S... COMING?!

TAK

!

BRIGHT!!

FLZ

WHAT'S WITH THIS LIGHT?!!

BUT...

HE GOT US. HE'S TAKEN HIS COMPANIONS AWAY.

HE SEEMS INTERESTING... I MEAN, TOUGH.

LIGHT MAGIC FASTER THAN MINE... WAS HE THE ENEMY BOSS?

EVERYBODY'S GONE!!

DAAAZE

...

WE MANAGED TO KEEP ONE.

BUT YOU'RE **ALWAYS** DOING THAT!!

SOME-THING REALLY AWFUL HAPPENED HERE...

HELLO THERE, MARX.

SORRY ABOUT THAT. THINGS GOT A BIT BUSY, AND I BLOCKED THE COMMUNICATION SPELL.

HM.

VWUM

I FINALLY GOT THROUGH! WHERE ARE YOU, WIZARD KING?!

YES, BUT... NEVER MIND THAT, JUST COME TO THE MEDICAL WARD!

THE CAPITAL WAS ATTACKED, CORRECT?

HUH ?!

AND YOU REPELLED THEM SAFELY, CORRECT?

HUH ?!

!

THIS MAGIC... IT'S...?!

FUEGO-LEON...

LEO...

WE SHOULD BE ALL RIGHT NOW.

SH

WE'VE STRENGTHENED THE MAGIC BARRIER, REPAIRED THE COMMUNI-CATION SPELLS AND MUSTERED MORE MAGIC KNIGHTS.

GOOD WORK, EVERYONE.

YO!

WUM

WSSH

!!

H...HEY, GUYS. YOU'RE ALL HERE.

AND...

...ASTA?!

YOU'RE OKAY?!

MURMUR

THE...

AND... AN ENEMY?!

THE WIZARD KING?!

BOOM

ASTAAAAAA!

DID THAT TEACH YOU ANYTHING, DORK-STA?!

THANK GOODNESS!

FIDGET FIDGET

MAN... I REALLY THOUGHT I WAS A GONER.

YOU'RE ALWAYS RECKLESS! THAT'S WHY THAT HAPPENED!

BOOM

ASTAAAAAA!

Y...YEAH. THANKS FOR WORRYING ABOUT ME.

...

GKH

I'M SO... SO GLAD YOU CAME BACK ALIVE!!

I WAS SURE YOU WERE DEAD... I'M SO GLAD!!

OW OW OW

TA·K TA·K TA·K

oh! I-I beg your pardon!

Wh... whub...

...

SQUEEZE

GLOMP

I WAS REALLY... REALLY WORRIED!!

ONE AS STRONG AS FUEGOLEON...

...AND THEY DON'T EVEN KNOW WHEN HE'LL WAKE UP.

I'M AFRAID I MISCALCULATED THERE.

I SEE...

WIZARD KING...

NO...

IT WAS DUE TO OUR INEXPERIENCE.

WAS THAT... WHAT THEY WERE AFTER?

WHO ON EARTH ARE THEY?

...THAT THE PENDANT FUEGOLEON WORE SEEMS TO BE GONE.

WE CONFIRMED...

...THINGS LOOK A BIT MORE COMPLICATED THAN THAT.

HM...

FROM WHAT THEY SAY, THEY SEEM TO BE A TERRORIST GROUP WITH A GRUDGE AGAINST THE KINGDOM, BUT...

THEY MIGHT HAVE GONE AFTER FUEGOLEON BECAUSE HE HAD THAT JEWEL, BUT...

...THE GREATER POSSIBILITY MAY BE THAT HIS STRENGTH AND IDEALS WOULD HAVE KEPT THEM FROM THEIR GOAL.

THE JEWELS EMBEDDED IN THAT STONE SLAB...

THERE WERE STILL SEVERAL OPEN SPACES. WHAT WILL HAPPEN WHEN THE JEWELS ARE ALL IN PLACE?

WAS FUEGOLEON'S PENDANT ONE OF THOSE?

WE'LL GET THE DETAILS FROM THE CAPTIVE LATER.

MAYBE I SHOULDN'T HAVE LEFT THE CAPITAL.

I'VE BEEN INVESTIGATING SEVERAL DISSIDENTS IN SECRET. THIS TIME, FOR THE FIRST TIME, I PICKED UP THEIR TRACKS AND WAS SEARCHING FOR THEM, BUT...

IN ANY CASE...

IF THEY'RE PLANNING SOMETHING EXTRAORDINARY WITH POWER THAT ENORMOUS...

PEOPLE LOOK TO THE MAGIC KNIGHTS FOR ONE THING—THE PEACE OF THE KINGDOM.

IN ORDER TO PRESERVE THAT, WE'LL KEEP FIGHTING WITH EVERYTHING WE HAVE.

WHAT'S WITH HIM? WE'RE SUPPOSED TO BE SHOWING SOLIDARITY RIGHT NOW! READ THE ATMOSPHERE, MAN!

...

SHUF

IF YOU'LL EXCUSE ME...

...

NOZEL!

AND...

PITIFUL... WHAT AN APPALLING SPECTACLE!!

NEVER LET THIS HAPPEN AGAIN, NOZEL!

...AND BURY THEM MYSELF!!

I WILL FIND THE SCUM WHO DID THIS TO YOU...

YOU SAID IT!

EITHER WAY... I'D RATHER NOT END UP FEELING THIS USELESS AGAIN.

?

HAS THE ENEMY AWAKENED NOT A SLEEPING LION, BUT A HAWK...?

WE...

...WILL GET STRONGER AS WELL!!

I'M THE ONE...WHO'S GOING TO GET STRONGEST!!

!

YOU NEED TO REST!!

LEOPOLD!

AND...

...I EXPECT YOU TO GET STRONGER TOO!!

YOU'RE MY RIVAL. WE FACED DEATH TOGETHER AND SURVIVED, AND SO...

ASTA! I'M GLAD WE BOTH PULLED THROUGH!!

"IT'S WORN ONLY BY THOSE PREPARED TO CONQUER THEMSELVES AND BECOME KING!"

"WHOA! THAT'S REALLY COOL!"

"IT'S A MARK HANDED DOWN IN THE VERMILLION FAMILY—THE SIGN OF A PERSONAL OATH.

"HM? AH, THIS...?

"BIG BROTHER! WHAT'S THAT MARK ON YOUR FOREHEAD?"

I'LL WORK HARD TOO, SO I'LL BE FIT TO BE HIS LITTLE BROTHER!!

WHOA!! AMAZING!! MY BROTHER IS SERIOUSLY AWESOME!!

HE JUST MIGHT BE THE ONE TO OBTAIN THE THRONES OF BOTH KING AND WIZARD KING, AND BECOME THE TRUE KING!

MASTER FUEGOLEON HAS BECOME A TRULY SPLENDID INDIVIDUAL!

I'LL BECOME A MAN...

...WHO SURPASSES EVEN FUEGOLEON!!!

VNNN

?!

...IS THE MARK OF MY OATH!!

THIS...

BOOM

NO... IT'S NOT THAT I WANT TO BE LIKE HIM.

...THE NEXT WIZARD KING!!!

I'LL BE THE ONE TO BECOME...

HUUUUUH?!

SO, WHO THE HECK ARE YOU ANYWAY?!

...BUT YOU LOOK LIKE YOU'LL MAKE A DECENT RIVAL!

HEH HEH

WHOA!

I DON'T REALLY GET IT...

WHA... THIS GUY MOVES WAY TOO FAST!!

WE'RE GONNA BE FRIENDS, SO CALL ME LEO!!

I DON'T WANT TO HEAR THAT FROM YOU!

I'M LEOPOLD VERMILLION!!

I ONLY REMEMBER GUYS WHO ACTUALLY INTRODUCE THEM-SELVES!!

HEY!! HOW CAN YOU STILL NOT KNOW THAT?!

HO HO HO HO

HAW HAW

TEE HEE

...AND DECLARED HIS INTENT TO CONTINUE RESOLUTELY OPPOSING THEM.

THE WIZARD KING CONCLUDED THAT THE ATTACK ON THE CAPITAL HAD BEEN THE WORK OF ANTI-CLOVER KINGDOM TERRORISTS...

HAD THE ENEMY DONE AWAY WITH THEM...OR HAD THEY DEFECTED?

THE ENEMY'S INVASION WAS ENABLED BY THE DISAPPEARANCE OF SOME OF THE MAGES WHO MAINTAINED THE CAPITAL'S MAGIC BARRIER.

THE KING'S SUPPORTERS PRESSED HIM REGARDING RESPONSIBILITY FOR THE DAMAGE.

EVEN SO, HE HAD GREAT SUPPORT AMONG THE PEOPLE, AND EXPECTATIONS FOR THE MAGIC KNIGHTS' ACTIVITY ROSE.

I DON'T WANT TO BELIEVE IT, BUT...

...BUT THE WIZARD KING WAS SURE OF IT.

THIS FACT WAS NOT MADE PUBLIC...

SO THAT ANTI-MAGIC KID'S NAME IS ASTA, HUH?

I'll muster the ultimate corpse army!!

That Asta punk... I swear I'm gonna slaughter him!!

GRIT GRIT

BESIDES, I HEALED YOUR WOUNDS, SO THERE'S NO WAY THEY HURT NOW.

Shaddup!! They ache, all right?!

I CAN'T HEEEAR YOU! I HOPE WE MEET AGAIN SOON, ASTA.

I saw that brat first!! Keep your mitts off him, Sally!!

UNTIL THEN...

DON'T YOU DARE KILL HIM, RADES!

I WANT TO TINKER WITH HIM WHILE HE'S STILL ALIVE.

I'LL USE THE LITTLE SAMPLES I GOT WHILE YOU WERE IN THE GEL...

...AND RESEARCH, RESEARCH, RESEARCH! ♪

...GEORK AND CATHERINE...

I COULDN'T SAVE...

SHUF

I'M NOT WORRIED ABOUT THAT.

AS LONG AS THEY'RE ALIVE...

...WE'LL RESCUE THEM WITHOUT FAIL!

THOSE TWO HAVE BIG EGOS, BUT THEY WORSHIP YOU.

THEY WON'T LEAK ANY OF OUR INFORMATION.

STILL... WE'LL BUILD UP OUR STRENGTH...

I THOUGHT I HAD DODGED IT... BUT I SEEM TO HAVE TAKEN A LITTLE OF THE ATTACK.

...AND WE WILL BRING HIM DOWN...

MAGIC THAT ACCELERATES THE FLOW OF TIME... DRASTICALLY! THE WIZARD KING... HE REALLY DOES HAVE PHENOMENAL POWER.

BOOM

...IN ORDER TO GET OUR REVENGE ON THE CLOVER KINGDOM...

...AND ESTABLISH A NEW COUNTRY THAT'S OURS ALONE!!

EVEN IF THERE WEREN'T, WE'D NEVER TALK!

THE MASTER IS THE LIGHT IN THE DARK-NESS!

OUR GOD!!

THERE'S A PROTECTION SPELL ON THEM. I CAN'T SEARCH FOR INFORMATION!

IT'S NO GOOD!!

I COULD TAKE ONE OF THOSE FOR YOU TOO.

THERE, THERE. JUST TRY THIS.

La?

THANK YOU!

WE'RE LOST!! HUGE!! THE CAPITAL'S HUGE!!

YOU'RE PROBABLY TOO YOUNG FOR THESE THINGS.

I HAD A FATEFUL ENCOUNTER.

BLISS

?

My! This is delicious.

WHERE YUMMY THINGS ARE, THERE I AM.

Laaa la la la la! Laa la la-la

AND ACTUALLY, WHY ARE YOU HERE, MIZ CHARMY?

YOU'RE IN A PRETTY GOOD MOOD, AREN'T YOU?

SERI-OUSLY?

HER MAGIC MAY ACTUALLY BE REALLY FANTASTIC...

!!

SQUISH SQUISH

POOF

POOF

POOF

POOF

LIKE THIS.

HOW DID YOU GET INTO THE NOBLE REALM?

HUH?

SHUP

HM?

WELL, IF IT ISN'T ASTA AND COMPANY.

THAT'S—!

HEEEEEY!!

HEY! *YUNO!!*

GIMME A PROPER GREETING, JERKFACE!!

Wait, you know him?!

Oh! The meal-saving prince?

...

YUNOOO! I HEAR YOU TOOK DOWN AN ENEMY LIKE IT WAS NOTHING, YOU JERK!

ARE YOUR INJURIES HEALED ALREADY? I ASKED YOU THAT BEFORE, DIDN'T I?

ASTAAA?

HM?

OOOWH

HM?

COURTESY MAKES THE WORLD GO ROUND, YOU KNOW!

DON'T GET SNOBBY JUST CUZ YOU TOOK ONE DOWN!

...

WHIRRRR

BWOOOOM

...

WAS HE TRYING TO KILL US OR SOMETHING?!

IS HE AN IDIOT...?

HM...?

FWIIIISH

WHAT DO YOU THINK YOU'RE DOING, YUNO?!

HUH? WAS THAT TOO MUCH?

...

WHOO, THAT MISSION WIPED ME OUT!!

THAT'S RIGHT, MAGNA!! LET'S SPRINT AHEAD WITH OUR COMBO MOVE, *CRACKLING MAGNA TYPHOON!!*

CRACKLING MAGNA TYPHOON!!

I'M NEVER DOING THAT MOVE AGAIN!!

BUT CHECK THIS OUT! THEY RECOGNIZED OUR DEEDS WITH A STAR!!

I'M GONNA KEEP RIGHT ON SHOWING THE OTHER BLACK BULLS HOW IT'S DONE, SUCKERS!!

HEY, ASTA! YOU'RE BACK TOO, HUH? BET YOU HAD IT ROUGH. BUT FROM NOW ON, THE ERA'S ALL MINE.

Wa ha ha!

WELCOME BACK, MAGNA AND LUCK!!

Gnrrrrgh! What's with that weird dance?

TATUM TATUM

Laa laa laa laa laaaa!

Worship me.

She just wanted to beat her up, but...

APPARENTLY THEY WERE IMPRESSED THAT SHE CAPTURED ONE OF THE REBELS.

FUEGO-LEON?

HM?

BUT... CAPTAIN FUEGOLEON GOT...

...

WA HA HA HA

IN ANY CASE, WELL DONE, KID.

HE'LL PROBABLY JUST LEVEL UP AND COME RIGHT BACK.

THAT HOT-BLOODED KING OF THE HARDNOSES WON'T DIE THAT EASY.

WHO DO YOU THINK YOU'RE WORRYING ABOUT, PUNK?

AWRIGHT!! THEN I'LL GO TRAIN AND LEVEL UP TOO!!

YEAH, YOU'RE RIGHT!!

NOPE.

YOU'RE ON VACATION, ASTA?!

IN THAT CASE...

FLINCH

REST...

Whoa...

What're you, an idiot?

BUT YOU MADE ME DO IT IN THE FIRST PLACE, CAPTAIN...

YOU REST.

YOU'LL MAKE YOUR INJURIES WORSE AND DIE.

A... MIXER?!!

BAAAM

BAAAM

LET'S HEAD TO A MIXER!!

YOU GET TO WORK.

63

✿ Page 38: The One I've Set My Heart On

WELL, LET'S GET THE INTRODUCTIONS STARTED. ♪

CHATTER

YAY

CHARMED!

FINRAL ROULACASE!!

TWENTY-ONE YEARS OLD, FROM TOUTA. I'M THE BLACK BULLS' SPATIAL MAGIC USER...

OOOOH!!

I'LL GO FIRST.

!

THAT'S AMAZING! THESE FLOWERS ONLY BLOOM ON MOUNT ANAHU, AND ONLY AT NIGHT, RIGHT?!

YAY

YAY

THEY'RE FRESH-PICKED MOON BLOSSOMS. PLEASE ACCEPT THEM AS A TOKEN OF OUR FRIENDSHIP. ♪

GO ON. WE'RE INTRODUCING OURSELVES!

DUUUUH

GOOD, I'VE GOT 'EM HOOKED!! THIS TIME I WILL GET A GIRLFRIEND!! AND IN ORDER TO MAKE THAT HAPPEN, I NEED ASTA AND LUCK TO GIVE IT ALL THEY'VE GOT TOO!!

I LIKE FIGHTING TOUGH ENEMIES IN BLOODY MORTAL COMBAT!!

KRAK

KRAK

LUCK VOLTIA, AGE 18, FROM IBON. I BELONG TO THE BLACK BULLS.

SO... I JUST HAVE TO SAY WHAT I LIKE, RIGHT?

UMMM... IN THE FUTURE, MY DREAM IS TO BECOME THE WIZARD KING!!

KRIK

KRIK

I-I-I- I'M ASTA!! I'M 15!! I'M FROM HAGE!! I'M A BLACK BULL!!

A MAN SHOULD TALK ABOUT HIS DREAM, RIGHT...?

...DICEY.

THESE TWO SEEM KINDA...

THERE'S NO WAY, HE'LL BECOME THE WIZARD KING. AND GEEZ, HE'S JUST A KID.

BESIDES, HAGE? HE'S A PEASANT! HE'S A SUPER-ULTRA PEASANT!

AND ACTUALLY, I HAD HEARD THEY'D BE MAGIC KNIGHTS... BUT THEY'RE BLACK BULLS?! THE BOTTOM OF THE HEAP?!

ALL RIGHT, IT'S YOUR TURN! INTRODUCE YOURSELVES, PLEASE.

NOT GOOD... LOOKS LIKE THAT DIDN'T GO OVER SO WELL.

YOU SAID IT!

HIGHER INCOME IS AN OBVIOUS MUST, BUT IF WE'RE ALSO TALLER AND OLDER THAN THEY ARE, THERE'S JUST NO WAY.

REBECCA. I WORK AT A RESTAURANT.

I WORK AS A HAIRDRESSER. I'M HELENE.

I'M ERIKA. I WORK AT A DRESSMAKER'S.

UMM... WE'RE ALL FRIENDS...

They're clearly losing interest...

YES, I WANT TO HEAR TOO!

NEVER MIND US! TELL US ABOUT THE MAGIC KNIGHTS!

HUH? AW, THAT'S REALLY NICE OF YOU!! IN THAT CASE, UM..

I'D LOVE TO HEAR ABOUT YOUR WORK.

WOW... YOU'VE ALL GOT SOLID JOBS. THAT'S FANTASTIC!

THE OTHER DAY, I SLAUGHTERED A GROUP OF TEN BANDITS!

Man, was that fun.

SNAP!

I KNOW! YOU'VE BEEN WORKING HARD LATELY, LUCK.

WHAT SORT OF JOBS HAVE YOU DONE?

Y-YESSIR!

SAY! ASTA, YOU PROTECTED THE CITIZENS OF THE CAPITAL, DIDN'T YOU?!

Well done!

BLANCH

THEY PUT THREE HOLES IN ME.

EXCEPT...

I DIDN'T MANAGE TO PROTECT MYSELF.

Seriously, it hurt like hell!

I GUESS HOLDING A MIXER WITH THESE GUYS REALLY WON'T WORK!!

ARRRRGH; THEY'RE USELESS!

BLANCH

YAMI HATES FLASHY PEOPLE, AND HE'D LECTURE THEM. WITH GREY, YOU CAN'T EVEN TELL WHICH ONE GREY IS, SO THAT WOULDN'T WORK.

I'll kill you.

WUZZAT?

? Sister

Sister Sister Sister

BUT THE OTHER GUYS ARE... WELL, MAGNA'S TOO MUCH OF A DELINQUENT. HE'D PUT THEM OFF. GAUCHE IS PRACTICALLY IN LOVE WITH HIS SISTER, AND HE'D PUT THEM OFF. GORDON IS TOO GLOOMY. HE'D PUT THEM OFF. AND ANYWAY, HE'S SCARY.

THERE ARE NO DECENT PEOPLE IN THE BLACK BULLS!!!

HEARING ABOUT THIS MIXER WORRIED ME SO MUCH I DISGUISED MYSELF AS AN EMPLOYEE AND CAME TO CHECK!

AGH, I CAN'T BELIEVE THIS. A MIXER! THIS IS EXACTLY WHAT'S WRONG WITH THOSE LOWBORN IMBECILES...

SHUF

CHATTER CHATTER

...

STILL, IT DOESN'T LOOK LIKE IT'S GOING WELL. THAT'S A RELIEF...

DON'T GET ME WRONG! IT'S NOT LIKE I CARE ABOUT THAT MUSCLE-BOUND SHRIMP.

IT DOESN'T MATTER WHO HE ENDS UP WITH OR WHAT THEY DO TOGETHER.

YOU KNOW THAT HUGE BLOWUP THEY HAD AT THE CAPITAL?

Say what?!

POUR IT YOURSELF, INSECT.

HEY, SISTER! GIMME A BEER!

HA HAR

THEY GAVE ME AN EXTRAORDINARY PROMOTION, AND I GOT BUMPED UP TO INTERMEDIATE MAGIC KNIGHT ALL AT ONCE (LIE). I TELL YOU... IT'S A PROBLEM. IT'S NOT LIKE I HAVE THAT MUCH TALENT, REALLY. (THIS IS TRUE.)

AS A MATTER OF FACT, I WAS *IN* THE CAPITAL, GUARDING A V.I.P. (LIE). I MANAGED TO TAKE OUT A FEW OF THE INVADERS (LIE)...

WHAT IS THIS? THE MIXER FROM HELL?

BLAAAA

I WAS NOT! WHAT'RE YOU TALKING ABOUT?!

HUH?!

OH. AND WHAT WERE YOU DOING THEN? YOU WERE READING A GIRLIE MAG, RIGHT?

WHAT'S WRONG? DOES BEING AROUND US INTIMIDATE YOU?

CHATTER

YOU THERE, WAITRESS! ANOTHER DRINK!!

POINT

I, SEKKE, TERRIFY MYSELF!!

THIS GUY... WAIT... WHO WAS HE?

CHATTER CHATTER CHATTER

BOOME

HAR

WHO'D HAVE IMAGINED MY BRONZE MAGIC WAS SO FORMIDABLE?

UH-OH... AM I STARTING TO LIKE BAD BOYS?!

HE'S GOT A CUTE SMILE, BUT THERE'S DANGER BEHIND IT... THAT'S ACTUALLY NOT BAD.

HUH? OH. WHY, SURE...

IT DOESN'T TAKE MUCH MAGIC, BUT YOU MUST NEED REALLY GOOD CONTROL! SHOW ME MORE!

WOW, SO THAT'S THE KIND OF SPELL YOU USE WHEN YOU CUT HAIR?!

HE'S A BIT FLASHY, AND HE'S NOT REALLY MY TYPE... BUT HE'S THE BEST ONE HERE! HE DOES SEEM TO BE SOME SORT OF NOBLE. SPATIAL MAGIC IS HANDY, AND HE'S CONSIDERATE AND KIND!

WOW... I THINK I'D LIKE THAT.

I'LL USE SPATIAL MAGIC AND WHISK YOU OVER TO IT NEXT TIME.

THE VIEW FROM THERE IS REALLY PRETTY.

WHAT'S WITH THIS LADY? SHE KEEPS LOOKING DOWN AND AWAY?! IS SHE MAD?! IS SHE MAD ABOUT SOMETHING?!

WHOA... THIS IS WAY AWKWARD!

YA

SHH

YA

...

WHAT'S YOUR FAVORITE FOOD?

UMM...

IT'S MY TURN!!

I don't really get it, but...

THAT'S NO GOOD! I'VE GOT TO IMPROVE THE MOOD!!

HAAAAH

ERIKA TOLD ME I SHOULD FIND A GOOD GUY FOR MY SIBLINGS' SAKE, SO I GOT DOLLED UP AND CAME ALONG, BUT...

I LEFT MY SIBLINGS AT HOME, AND I CAN'T QUIT WORRYING ABOUT THEM.

THIS ISN'T LIKE ME.

RUFFLE RUFFLE

YOU DON'T HAVE TO FORCE YOURSELF TO MAKE SMALL TALK.

I QUIT TOO. THIS IS DUMB.

!

OH! I HAVE FIVE SIBLINGS TOO. I MEAN, THEY'RE NOT REALLY SIBLINGS, BUT THEY'RE *LIKE* SIBLINGS.

THEY WERE ANNOYING SOMETIMES, BUT IT WAS FUN.

ONLY THEY'RE NOT WITH ME NOW...

SO YOU LIVE WITH YOUR SIBLINGS?!

YES. THREE LITTLE BROTHERS AND TWO LITTLE SISTERS.

YEAH, AND EVEN IF YOU CAN ACT LIKE A DORK AROUND YOUR FRIENDS, WHEN YOU'RE WITH YOUR SIBLINGS, YOU TRY TO ACT COOL...

I KNOW! IT'S ANNOYING WHEN THEY'RE THERE, BUT IT'S LONELY WHEN THEY'RE NOT!

I SLEEP BETTER NOW THAT THERE AREN'T ANY LITTLE KIDS IN THE BED, BUT IT'S KINDA LONELY...

AH HA HA! I KNOW!

HUUUUH?!

SILENCE, INSECT.

WHA... HEY, MISS! DON'T BREAK OUR PLATES!

YOU SAID YOU WANTED WORK ALL OF A SUDDEN, SO I HIRED YOU, BUT YOU'VE BEEN DOING A TERRIBLE JOB!

CRAAACK

BRR BRR

Hey! They are having fun!!

MAGIC KNIGHTS...

Hic... Hic!

YA LOOK LIKE YER HAVIN' FUN...

YOU KNOW, REBECCA, YOU DO LOOK LIKE A BIG-SISTER TYPE.

YOU DON'T LOOK LIKE AN OLDEST KID, THOUGH.

TOTTER

WELL, WELL.

TAKIN' AROUND A PRETTY LADY LIKE THIS... THAT'S REAL CLASSY.

IF A SHRIMP LIKE THIS CAN MAKE IT IN, MEBBE I'LL JOIN THE MAGIC KNIGHTS MYSELF.

HUH? WHA'S WITH THIS KID? ARE YA REALLY A MAGIC KNIGHT?

BET YOU'RE DESPERATE TO CATCH YOURSELF A MAGIC KNIGHT, AIN'TCHA, MISSY?

Heh heh! I'M PRETTY SURPRISED I GOT IN TOO.

AH! YOU'RE THE GIRL AT THE LOCAL RESTAURANT!

HMMMM?

THE ONE WHO CARRIES A LITTLE KID AND WORKS UNTIL SHE GETS ALL SWEATY EVERY SINGLE DAY!

HIC

Y'KNOW... I'VE SEEN YOU BEFORE...

NO... THEY'RE MY BROTHERS...

YOUR MAN RAN OUT ON YOU, DIDN'T HE!

ARE THOSE LI'L BRATS YOUR KIDS?

HAW HAW HAW HAW

MUTTER MUTTER

YEAH, I BET YOU DO WANNA LAND A MAGIC KNIGHT SO YOU CAN TAKE IT EASY!!

SQUEEZE

!

WHA...!

WAIT... LET ME GO!

GRAB

GWEH HEH HEH HEH HEH

IF YOU WANT TO GET A MAN THAT BAD, COME PLAY WITH ME.

WHOA?

WHUH?

TUG

HUP

WHAT KINDA AMAZIN' MAGIC ARE YA GONNA SHOW ME, LI'L MAGIC KNIGHT?

OOOOOH, SCARY...

DON'T JUDGE PEOPLE ON APPEAR- ANCES!!

YOU DON'T KNOW ANYTHING ABOUT THIS LADY!

Let's go home.

HAR ...

I'm quitting, manager!

Huh ?!

WHAT ARE YOU DOING?!

RUN!!

NAH, I'M SORRY FOR BUSTING UP THE MIXER!

...

THANKS, ASTA!

THAT FELT GREAT.

IS THERE... ANYBODY YOU LIKE?

SAY, ASTA?

...

...

WHAT ?!

YOU MEAN ...

HUH ?!

YES!! THERE'S SOMEBODY I'VE GOT MY HEART SET ON!!

YOU MEAN... COULD IT BE... IT COULDN'T BE...M... M-M-ME...

WILL DO!!

PLAY WITH MY BROTHERS AND SISTERS.

COME VISIT MY PLACE ONE OF THESE DAYS!!

I SEE. WELL, I'M ROOTING FOR YOU!!

JUST BECAUSE I'M ROOTING FOR HIM DOESN'T MEAN I'M GIVING UP.

HEH HEH HEH

SISTER!! SOMEDAY I'LL BECOME THE WIZARD KING, AND THEN I'LL COME TO GET YOU!!

NO... NO-NO-NO! EVEN IF IT IS, SO WHAT?! IT'S NOT AS IF I-I-I-I...

I GOT DUMPED...

I knew it. The Black Bulls are barbarians.

HUH?!

BY THE WAY, WHAT DO PEOPLE GO TO MIXERS FOR, ANYWAY?

Rebecca Scarlet

Age: 16
Height: 165 cm
Birthday: April 18
Sign: Aries
Blood Type: A
Likes: Her brothers and sisters, cooking

WELL, NOW.

Too... strong...

What was that magic?!

✿ Page 39: The Mirror Mage

I WON'T KILL YOU THIS TIME.

...

!

SHUF

BECAUSE TODAY...

Sp... spare us, please!! We'll stop attacking the village!

HOW DO YOU WANT TO DIE?

Yeek!

...IS MY LITTLE SISTER MARIE'S BIRTHDAY.

SNAP

HEH HEH HEH

DRIBBLE

GRIND

CELEBRATE LIKE CRAZY.

WITH EVERYTHING YOU'VE GOT.

THEN DIE.

GRIND

SO WE'RE DYING ANY-WAY?!

GRIND GRIND

WHO'S THAT KID?!

GO ON.

YOU WISH MARIE A HAPPY BIRTHDAY TOO, SCUM.

HUH?

MY DEAR, BELOVED SISTER MARIE.

I'VE JUST ARRIVED IN THE COMMON REALM TOWN OF NEAN, WHERE YOU LIVE.

A MAGIC KNIGHT'S WORK IS HARD, BUT IF IT'S FOR YOU, I FEEL NO PAIN.

YOUR BIG BROTHER JUST FINISHED A JOB.

IT'S ALL FOR YOUR SAKE, AND IT'S ALL THANKS TO YOU. YOU, MARIE, WHO ARE AS SWEET AS AN ANGEL INCARNATE.

I, A FORMER PRISONER, AM NOW LIVING A DECENT LIFE.

AH... MY NOSE- BLEED IS ALREADY UNSTOP- PABLE...

I BOUGHT LOTS OF TOYS I THOUGHT YOU'D LIKE, SO PLEASE BE HAPPY.

AND EVEN SO, I'M LATE, BUT PLEASE FORGIVE ME.

SHUF

SHUF

THIS DAY, THE DAY I'M ABLE TO SPEND WITH YOU, IS SACRED.

LOADED

WAH HA HA HA HA

WAH HA HA HA HA

FOOM   FOOM

HM?

I KNOW THAT MORONIC FACE.

WHEE WHEE

THAT'S OUR NEW GUY. UH... PASTA?

YAAAAY!

OKAAAAY! YOU'RE NEXT, MARIE!

WHUNK

DOOOOOOM

WHO HAS A NOSEBLEED AND A SISTER COMPLEX, YOU MUSCLE-BOUND RUNT?

I'LL STOMP YOU TO DEATH.

OH! YOU'RE... THE SENIOR MEMBER WITH THE NOSEBLEED AND THE SISTER COMPLEX!

GRIND GRIND

AAAAAH

You get away from her this instant, trash!!

AAAAAAAH

GRIND GRIND GRIND

BAAAM

GRRR...

I'M IN GREAT SHAPE, SO YOU'LL HAVE TO DO MORE THAN THAT!!

HA HA HA HA!

SO THIS IS YOUR LITTLE SISTER, MISTER GONZALES?!

Who are you calling Gonzales?! It's Gauche, you moron!

And I know I showed you Marie's photo, Pasta.

I'M NOT PASTA! I'M ASTA!

Today is the day I get to unleash those pent-up feelings, worship the heck out of my little sister and be all over her, so why are you here worshipping her first, huh?!

Doing thiiis, and thaaat...

THERE, SEE? HE DOES HAVE A NOSEBLEED AND A SISTER COMPLEX.

The church in this town cares for my little sister. I only get to see her once a month.

DRIP

DRIP

DRIP

THOOM

Keep your hairy eyeballs off my sister. You pervert.

What else would she be, scumbag?

STOP IT!

HELLO.

MARIE'S REALLY CUTE!

He's scary

See...

REBECCA FROM THE RESTAURANT HERE IS MY FRIEND. I JUST CAME BY TO PLAY.

I'M GOING TO MARRY HIM!!

BIG BROTHER, DON'T BE MEAN TO ASTA!

KRIK

HUH?

WHAT?

BOOOM

MARRY HIM?!!

Secretly Followed Asta

SNEAK

KRAAAK

NOOOOOO!

AAAAAAH!!

KIIIIIIILL!

YAAAAAAGH!!

BRR BRR BRR

PLOPP!

I'll kill you...!!

IT'S RATHER NOISY OUT HERE, ISN'T IT?

WELL, WELL. YOU'RE HERE, GAUCHE?

OLD HAG...!

NOT "OLD HAG." CALL ME "SISTER."

IT'S TIME. WE NEED TO GO BACK TO THE CHURCH NOW.

SISTER!

MARIE!

NO CAN DO. IT'S TIME.

YOU GO HOME, YOU SISTER-COMPLEX PUNK.

MARIE'S GOING ON A DATE WITH ME.

GO HOME BY YOURSELF, OLD SISTER HAG.

YOUR ATTITUDE'S ALWAYS TERRIBLE, YOU HAVE MEAN EYES AND A FILTHY MOUTH...

IN ANY CASE, IT'S NOT GOOD FOR MARIE TO SPEND TIME WITH A FELLOW LIKE YOU.

I WHAT, YOU DAMN HAG?!

SHADDUP, *GANGSTER HAG.*

YEAH, RIGHT, *MORON.* YOU LOOK LIKE YOU COULD LIVE ANOTHER HUNDRED YEARS, YOU OLD SHE-GHOUL.

HOW CAN YOU SAY THAT TO AN OLD LADY WHO'S NOT LONG FOR THIS WORLD, YOU *FOOL?*

YOU SEE? FILTHY.

DON'T TALK ABOUT PEOPLE LIKE THEY'RE MONSTERS, *THUG.*

SHADDUP. *DIE.*

IN ANY CASE, GO HOME.

COME ALONG, MARIE.

Don't butt in when we're talking!

MISTER GAUCHE! YOU SHOULDN'T TALK TO THE ELDERLY LIKE THAT!!

Ma... Ma-riiiiiiiie!

AAAAUGH

BROTHER! ASTA! SEE YOU LATER!

It's not nice!

BAAAM

WELL... DO YOU TWO WANT TO SPEND THE NIGHT AT MY PLACE?

CAN WE?!

...

SEE YA!

HE JUST **MET** THE WOMAN, AND HE'S SPENDING THE NIGHT AT HER HOUSE? IS HE AN IDIOT?! SERIOUSLY, IS HE?!

I WONDERED WHERE HE WAS GOING ON HIS VACATION, SO I FOLLOWED HIM, BUT... THAT'S THE LADY FROM THE MIXER, ISN'T IT?!

...

SPEND THE NIGHT?!

SPUH... SP- SP- SP...

YOU'RE GOING TO MAKE SOMEBODY A REAL GOOD WIFE, REBECCA!

HA HA HA HA

HUH ?!

REALLY? THAT'S GREAT.

YUUUUM!

YUH...

ISN'T IT?

NO, NO! STUPID, STUPID, STUPID!

JUMP HIM...?! SNEAK INTO HIS ROOM...?!

BADMP BADMP BADMP

SIS, GO ON AND JUMP ASTA TONIGHT.

YOU IDIOT! WHAT ARE YOU SAYING, LUCA?!

BIG SIS, ARE YOU MARRYIN' ASTA?

WHA...?! NO, MARCO!

ASTA...

SNOOORE

CREEEEAK

SNRRR

FLIP

Die,
Asta.

WACHOO

WAH AH...

ROCLLLS...

Mirror
Magic:

Reflect
Ray

Real Double

YOUR CRIME...

AND A BEAM CAME OUT OF THAT MIRROR... WHAT'S WITH THIS GUY'S MAGIC?!

THERE'S... TWO GAUCHES?!!

...IS HAVING MET MY SISTER.

...PRETTY MUCH EVERY-BODY'S A CRIMINAL!!

RAAAAAH

SPAK SPAK

SPAK

BUT THAT MEANS...

?!

HUH?

SHUT UP AND DIE.

Gweh!!

This isn't our house!!

OH, REBECCA!

I'm really sorry!

WHA...?! WHAT ARE YOU TWO DOING?!

DWARRRRGH!

DIE.

NOBODY CARES.

SUH... SNOW?!

WHEN DID ALL OF THIS...

I MEAN, ISN'T IT STILL TOO EARLY FOR...?!

THE KIDS ARE GONE!!

HUH...?!

NOW'S NOT THE TIME FOR THAT!

✤ Page 40: Pursuit over the Snow

THE KIDS...

THEY'RE GONE!!

MAYBE THE BATHROOM?

LUCA AND MARCO... WHERE COULD THEY BE AT THIS HOUR?

FAWN IS GONE!!

CHRIS ?!

URIAN, WHERE ARE YOU?

!

101

HUH?

HEY! WHAT'S WRONG WITH THIS TOWN?!

WHAT IN THE WORLD...?!

Die.

Get over it already!

DWAA-AAH!

NOT THE BATHROOM, I GUESS.

I SAW LOTS OF CHILDREN LEAVE FOR THE MOUNTAIN ALL OF A SUDDEN A LITTLE WHILE AGO.

WHAT WAS THAT? MAGIC? SOME KIND OF FESTIVAL??

C... COLD...

NOELLE ?!

SNOW FALLING OUT OF NOWHERE AT THIS TIME OF YEAR? THAT'S INSANE!!

THIS SNOW...

I SENSE MAGIC. SOMEONE'S SPELL.

BY THE WAY, NOELLE, WHAT'RE YOU DOING HERE?

I... JUST HAPPENED TO BE PASSING THROUGH!

YOU MEAN...!

HEY, OLD HAG...

YOU SAID SEVERAL KIDS WERE TAKEN.

DON'T TELL ME...

MARIE BETTER NOT HAVE BEEN ONE OF THEM!!

A SPELL THAT CONTROLS ITS TARGETS. IT MAY BE LIMITED TO CHILDREN WHOSE MAGIC HASN'T DEVELOPED YET.

SEVERAL OF OURS WERE TAKEN AS WELL!

KIDNAPPING CHILDREN... WHAT DO THEY PLAN TO DO WITH THEM?!

SHUF

UNFORTUNATELY, YES!

...

GRRRT
GRRRT

You were **right** there, hag!

GRRRT

What were you doing?!

AB

GROLDHAAAG!

STOP, PLEASE!!

...

YOU'RE RIGHT.

IF YOU WANT TO HIT ME, GO AHEAD, BUT IT WON'T BRING THE CHILDREN BACK!!

RESORTING TO VIOLENCE IMMEDIATELY...! YOU REALLY ARE A GOOD-FOR-NOTHING!!

SISTER THERESA!

But I've got to vent this anger somehow!!

!!

JUST CALM DOWN A LITTLE...

NOW, NOW, MISTER GAUCHE.

ASTA...

YOU LITTLE ....!!

105

...ALL RIGHT ?!!

A MAGIC KNIGHT...

...

...SHOULD ALWAYS KEEP A COOL HEAD!!

NO, BUT LISTEN, LET'S FORGET ABOUT THIS AND JUST GO LOOK FOR CLUES!

That hurt, you lousy brat!!

AAAAAH!

OH...

I over-did it!

BA DMP BA DMP

I'll kill you calmly!!

...

TEETER

YOU'RE RIGHT.

ALL RIGHT!

THAT'S IT!

That aside, I'm killing you!!

Say what ?!

IF I USE THE TRANSMISSION SPELL THAT LINKS US TO LOOK FOR THE MANA IN THE MIRROR, I'LL BE ABLE TO TELL ROUGHLY WHERE SHE IS!!

I HAVE MARIE CARRY A MAGIC MIRROR WITH HER EVERY-WHERE.

NO. SHE'S ANNOYING, BUT THAT OLD HAG PACKS SOME POWER.

SISTER GRANNY! JUST LEAVE IT TO US...

HUH ?

SHUF

WE'LL MAKE THEM GIVE BACK THE CHURCH'S CHILDREN.

I'LL GO AS WELL.

ASTA ...!

108

OH... WHAT WILL I DO?! IF ANYTHING HAPPENS TO THEM...

SNIFF SNIFFLE

MARCO'S DUMB, AND LUCA HAS A STUBBORN STREAK. I'M WORRIED...

DON'T WORRY!

Hiyah!

SNAP OUT OF IT, REBECCA!

IF YOU'RE PANICKING WHEN WE GET BACK, YOU'RE GONNA GET LAUGHED AT.

I'M ABSOLUTELY, POSITIVELY GONNA BRING 'EM BACK!!

LET'S GO.

THE TOWN MIGHT STILL GET ATTACKED. YOU STAY HERE AND PROTECT IT.

YOU CAN'T FLY ON YOUR OWN, RIGHT? YOU WANNA HANG LIKE THIS GUY?

WAIT! I'M COMING TOO!!

I'm staying behind with this woman...?!

...

REPORT THIS TO THE MAGIC KNIGHTS.

WHROOSH

OH, WOW!

EVERYONE'S SPACING OUT, AND THEY CAN'T TALK.

IS THAT THE PERSON WHO BROUGHT US HERE?

!

HMMM?

I WONDER WHY.

MY MAGIC WORE OFF ON YOU.

THE MIRROR MY BROTHER GAVE ME... HE SAID IT PROTECTS ME FROM MAGIC, JUST A LITTLE.

IS THAT WHY I'M OKAY?

Think of that mirror as me.

NO...

PUTTING A SPELL ON PEOPLE AND MAKING THEM DO WHAT YOU WANT...

IF YOU DON'T, WE CAN'T BE FRIENDS.

YOU'RE A BAD GIRL. YOU HAVE TO BE GOOD AND STAY UNDER MY SPELL.

WHY...

WHY ARE YOU SO MEAN?

THAT'S NOT A REAL FRIEND.

!!

SMACK

WHROOMH

A friend wouldn't say things like that!!

SHUK

DON'T DAMAGE THE MER- CHANDISE!

NIEGE!

SHUFF

HAAAH HAAAH

...XMMM

Yeesh... You're a real piece of work.

I... I'm sorry, big brother...

SHE'LL BE THE STAR ATTRACTION THIS TIME!

With this many of 'em, we'll make out like bandits.

HM...?

115

Gauche Adlai

Age: 19
Height: 181 cm
Birthday: June 27
Sign: Cancer
Blood Type: B
Likes: **Marie**

THEN THE KIDNAPPED CHILDREN ARE IN THOSE CAVES?!

I'M PICKING UP MANA FROM OVER THERE!!

HM?!

TAKE US DOWN A LITTLE, MISTER GAUCHE!

THAT KINDA LOOKS LIKE REBECCA'S BROTHER!!

THAT'S...

HWOO O

UH—

DWAAAAAAAAAAAAAAAH!!

HUP!

BAT!

NOT MY PROBLEM.

MARIE'S THE ONLY ONE I CARE ABOUT.

WHA?!

HWOO

Rrrrgh...

IF YOU WANT DOWN, THEN JUMP.

GAUCHE... YOU ARE UNBELIEV-ABLE!

WHROOSH

ASTA!!

SNAP OUT OF IT!

MARCO!

IT'S NO USE. HE'S UNDER A SPELL, AND HIS MIND ISN'T HERE!

HEY! MARCO!

THIS IS AWFUL... HE'S COVERED IN SCRAPES AND BRUISES, AND HE'S GETTING FROSTBITE!!

TONK

YOU OKAY, MARCO?!

HUH...?

ASTA... SISTER...

...

FLIP

GLOW

WAIT JUST A MOMENT!

!!

OWWWW!

WHAT ON EARTH WAS THAT...?!

HE ERASED THE SPELL?!

Sacred Healing Light **GLOOOo** Flame Recovery Magic:

HE'S HURT SO BAD...

I...I DUNNO...

WHAT IN THE WORLD HAPPENED?!

...

IT'S SO WAAARM...

NOOO! I'M SCARED, ASTA! STAY WITH ME!

...

HUH ?!

MARCO! WE HAVE TO GO SAVE YOUR BIG SIS AND THE OTHER KIDS!

CAN YOU WAIT IN THAT CAVE BY YOURSELF?

IT'S GOT MAGIC KNIGHT COURAGE IN IT!!

IF YOU WEAR THAT, YOU'LL BE FINE!

WELL, GUESS THERE'S NO HELPING IT! I'LL LET YOU BORROW MY BLACK BULLS ROBE, JUST THIS ONCE!!

WHAT'RE YOU TALKING ABOUT?! YOU'RE A GUY TOO, RIGHT?!

AND THAT'S JUST A LOAN, GOT IT?!

YOU'D BETTER GIVE IT BACK LATER!!

UH... UH-HUH!!

WE'LL BE BACK, SO YOU WAIT FOR US. ALL RIGHT?!

...

VWIII SHIIZZT

AAAAAH

Squeeze out more magic, kid!!

Gweh heh heh heh heh!! Good, that's real good!

NO... DON'T!

YOU MUSTN'T DISOBEY MY BROTHER!

MAYBE THE STAR ATTRAC- TION?

ALL RIGHT... NEXT...

FWUMP

AND SHE'S DONE.

Snow Cry

Snow Magic:

KAFOOM

MY ATTACKS ARE MISSING!

OOOH...

!!

Snow
Creation
Magic:

Snow
Friends

UPPITY
LITTLE
JERK!!

GO, MY
FRIENDS!

LOUSY FRIGGIN'...! WE HAVEN'T DRAINED ALL THE MAGIC YET!

AND ACTUALLY...

THAT MAN IS STRONG!

Also scary!

AAAAAH! MY FRIENDS...

FLUMP

FLUMP

SHADDUP, SLOWPOKE!! USE YOUR OWN BRAIN FOR A CHANGE!!

WHAT SHOULD I DO, BROTHER?!

RAAAAAAAARGH!

WHAT IS WITH THIS GUY'S MAGIC?!

HW

OOO

HOW COULD YOU DO SOMETHING THAT HORRIBLE?!

...

THEY MAY NEVER.. BE ABLE TO USE MAGIC AGAIN!

THESE CHILDREN... THEIR MAGIC'S BEEN EXTRACTED ?!

THIS GUY'S...

HUH?

DAMN IT... REINFORCEMENTS?!

A two-bit punk who's not even a Magic Knight!! I'll take you out my—

You've got **no** magic! Zip! Zilch! Nada!!

Gweh hee ha ha ha!! What's with **you**?!

Gwehhee
...

BLUGH

FWUMP

KROOO

★ Page 42: Three-Leaf Sprouts

*THAT BOY...
WHAT
STRENGTH!!*

....!!

I SEE...

THIS BOY IS...!

THAT... ISN'T MAGIC?!

I FELT SO LITTLE MAGIC FROM HIM THAT I WAS WORRIED, BUT...

OH

FLASH

AAAAAAAAAUGH!

!

REAL
DOUBLE.

HOWEVER,
GAUCHE'S MAGIC IS
EQUAL TO IT. MOST
OF ALL, HE'S GOOD
AT FIGHTING WITH
SPELLS! IT'S JUST
AS I THOUGHT.

THE YOUNG
CRIMINAL...
HE MADE
SNOW FALL
OVER A WIDE
AREA. HIS
POWER IS
STUPENDOUS.

I'D
ALREADY
ACTIVATED
IT, RIGHT
BEFORE YOU
CAUGHT ME.

MY *REAL
DOUBLE* IS A
SPELL THAT
SUMMONS
ANOTHER
ME OUT OF
THE MIRROR
WORLD.

HE'S
STRONG!!

What's Neige doing?

The guy's completely useless. Blasted...

...

...DID YOU DO SOMETHING THIS NASTY?!

WHY...

DO YOU?!

DO YOU EVEN KNOW HOW MUCH IT HURTS TO LOSE YOUR MAGIC?!

YOU'RE GONNA PAY FOR IT PROPERLY, STARTING NOW!!

THIS PAIN ISN'T ENOUGH TO MAKE UP FOR WHAT YOU DID!!

NEVER MIND HIM. WE HAVE TO DO SOMETHING ABOUT THE CHILDREN...

THAT'S RIGHT! A MAN LIKE THAT ISN'T EVEN WORTH STRIKING WITH YOUR FIST.

Rrgh...

Ghk...

OH! OH, YEAH!

...

TAAAAKE THAT 'N' THAT 'N' THAT 'N' THAT 'N' THAT!!

BONK

BONK

!

GLOOOOO

WAAAH

MOMMY! DADDY!

MY FEET HUUURT!

WHERE ARE WE?

SISTER!

ASTA!

LUCA!

THERE, THERE! ALL RIGHT, EVERYONE COME TO ME.

HUH ?!

HOW'D YOU KNOW ?!

DIDN'T YOU GROW UP IN THE CHURCH IN HAGE?

ASTA.

WE HAD A CHANCE TO TALK FOR THE FIRST TIME IN AGES, AND SHE TOLD ME ABOUT YOU.

THE SISTER TALKED ABOUT *ME*?! WHAT DID SHE SAY?!

SHE WAS A FINE YOUNG WOMAN.

ISN'T SHE?!

SISTER LILY FROM YOUR CHURCH CAME TO OURS TO TRAIN ONCE.

HUH?!

Whoa!

BOOONG

HEH HEH

BUT...

THAT YOU WERE A SMALL, NOISY CHILD.

...AND THAT SHE WAS VERY PROUD OF YOU.

SHE ALSO SAID YOU WERE A HARD WORKER WITH A STRONG HEART WHO WOULDN'T GIVE UP IN THE FACE OF ADVERSITY...

WAAAAUGH!

!

I WON'T GIVE UP ON YOU EITHER!!

SISTER...!!

HE CAN'T FIGHT ANYMORE!

GAUCHE, STOP THAT!

WHUD

Gkh!!

He hurt Marie.

The only way to atone for that is death!!

No, I can't.

I'm eliminating anyone who might hurt you right now!!

TH OOM THOOM

TWITCH

SO PLEASE FORGIVE HIM!

GAUCHE! I'M OKAY!! SISTER THERESA HEALED MY INJURIES TOO...

YOU TWO... WHY DID YOU DO THIS?!

NEVER MIND THAT! WE HAVE TO GET THEM TO TELL US HOW TO RETURN THE CHILDREN'S MAGIC!!

THEY'RE THE THREE-LEAF SPROUTS THAT GRACE THE NATION!

CHILDREN ARE THE VERY FUTURE OF THIS COUNTRY.

...

Uuuuuu ...

...

GOSH, YOU'RE WHINY AND LOUD.

I'LL GIVE YOU A PAT ON THE BACK THIS TIME, THOUGH!

THEY SHUT DOWN OUR MAGIC COLLECTING! HELP US!!

YOU'RE HERE, HUH?! IF YOU CAN TRAVEL WITH SPATIAL MAGIC, YOU SURE TOOK YOUR SWEET TIME!

...!

THAT'S...

SHUF

Gel Magic: Sticky Salamander

THEN DIE.

WOULD YOU NOT INTERRUPT OUR MOVING REUNION?

WHILE I'M AT IT... MAYBE I'LL DISSECT EVERYBODY...

This is the sort of classic among classics that makes you think, "Now this is *Shonen Jump* manga!" (ノ´・∀・)ノ
It's packed with friendship, hard work and victory! *Jump* kids, if you don't read this one, you'll spend your whole life missing out.

When I see Asta barreling straight ahead and working hard at everything without cutting corners, it makes me want to do my best too. I wish I had a little brother like him. (｡−∀−｡)

And check out the relationship between the "hot-blooded failure" Asta and his friend, the "coolheaded genius" Yuno!!! After all, in the sort of manga where the hero's aiming for the top (Wizard King), you've just got to have a rival!

He has all sorts of other unique companions too.
My particular favorite is Charmy Pappitson.♥
She looks unreliable, but she's actually superstrong, and on top of that, she's cute! It's not fair!
I heard she's modeled on Tabata-sensei's wife, and now I'm really curious. (−▼−)

Most of all, the art is pretty.☆
The drawings in every single panel are practically fine art, instead of comics. \ (o°w°o)/
Before now, I never cared about anything except the story of a manga, but after meeting *Black Clover*, I've started to pay attention to the art too.

Another great thing about it is all the amazing dialog that resonates with you! These are my personal top three:

1. Asta
"Gravel may be gravel, but me? I'm gravel that shatters diamonds!!!!"

2. Charmy
"I don't care who they are~ Nobody touches my food!"

3. Noelle
"It's your fault for standing there. Who gave you permission to be there?"

I really can't wait to find out what happens next. (^^)

I want to know how Noelle and Mimosa's loves are going to turn out too...♥

Honoka Akimoto

The center of the girls' high school idol singer group Team Shachihoko from Nagoya, affiliated with Section 3 of Stardust Promotion. Her image color is Nagoya Red. She's actually a huge *Black Clover* fan, and she sent us a special comment!

Page 43: Explosion of Malice

GET RID OF THEM!!

THESE GUYS GOT IN OUR WAY!!

THE EYE OF THE MIDNIGHT SUN!!

THE TERRORISTS WHO ATTACKED THE CAPITAL?!

WHAT IS THIS OMINOUS MAGIC?!

WELL, NOT THAT IT MATTERS ANYMORE.

Heh, heh, heh!

WHAT'S THIS? I CAME BECAUSE YOU CALLED ME WITH THE MAGIC TRANSMISSION ITEM, BUT YOU HAVEN'T COLLECTED MUCH MAGIC, HAVE YOU?

MISTER GAUCHE, GRANNY! BE CAREFUL!

I HEARD SHE BLOCKED THE SILVER TEAM CAPTAIN'S ATTACK TOO!

SHE BLOCKED GAUCHE'S MAGIC SO EASILY...

SO THEY'RE INVOLVED WITH THIS!

HERE I COME!!

HEH HEH HEH...

INCOM-ING!!

BLOOP

IF IT WERE MORE POWERFUL MAGIC, THINGS COULD BE DIFFERENT...

THAT'S SOME FIIINE MAGIC, BUT IT GETS REFRACTED INSIDE MISTER SALAMAN, SO THERE'S NOT MUCH POINT.

SHE WARPED ALL OF IT!!

SHLOooo

RIGHT?!

SWISH

UWOOP

WHAT THE?!

!

THAT'S NOT GONNA...

FOOM

TMP

SPL

AP

SPLAP

!!

GOTCHA!♪

UMP

WH

Dwah!!

HEH HEH HEH

I want to know...

...every-thing about you.

I wonder what's different?

I CAN'T MOVE!!

...

YOU *LOOK* JUST LIKE A NORMAL HUMAN.

That **hurt!!** And you're **scary!!**

WELL, YOUR BLOOD'S NORMAL.

LAP

LAP

MMMMM...

GYAAAH!!

CHOMP

RARR!

YAAAAAAGH

No!! Stop!!

OKAY, NEXT I'LL TAKE YOUR LITTLE FINGERNAIL.

HEH HEH HEH HEH HEH HEH HEH HEH

GRRT

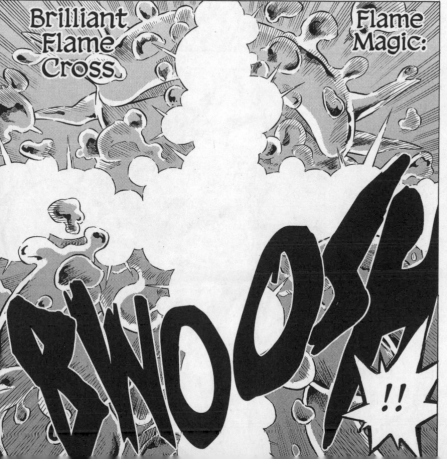

Brilliant Flame Cross

Flame Magic:

BWOOSH!!

SIZZ

FWOOSH

WHOA!

TMP

THAT'S ENOUGH OF THAT!

FOOOM

I WON'T GIVE YOU THIS BOY!!

Thanks!!

GRANNY!

YOU'RE REALLY TOUGH!!

YOU MELTED MISTER SALAMAN.

OH WOW...

THERESA, THE CRIMSON SHE-LEOPARD!! THAT'S ME!!

I MAY BE OLD, BUT I'M A FORMER MAGIC KNIGHT!!

BA M

CRIMSON... THEN, HEY, DO YOU KNOW CAPTAIN FUEGOLEON?!

FORMER MAGIC KNIGHT ?!

She's all pumped up!!

HUH ?!!

HE WAS A SNOT-NOSED KID, BUT HE GREW UP QUITE WELL!

...

Really can't picture that...

WHEN I SERVED AT THE PALACE, I WAS HIS TEACHER.

FUEGO... OH, FUEGGY. YES!

Fueggy ?!

WE WON'T FAIL...

WE'LL CATCH THIS ONE!!

YES... I KNOW.

BUT GRANNY...

RIGHT NOW, CAPTAIN FUEGO-LEON'S...

HEY, YOU!

THIS DOESN'T LOOK SO GOOD.

THREE AGAINST ONE, HUH?

164

WEEEELL...

THERE'S A WAY, YES, BUT...ARE YOU SURE?

YOU CAN DO THAT, RIGHT?!

WEEZ WEEZ

I'LL BACK YOU UP WITH MY AWESOME MUD MAGIC... SO FIX MY BODY SO I CAN MOVE!!

YEAH, RIGHT. ONCE I'M FIXED UP AND SHE FORKS OVER THE MONEY, I'M MAKING A BREAK FOR IT.

DO IT AND I'LL HELP YOU!!

YEAH, ANYTHING'S FINE. JUST HURRY UP AND HEAL ME!! THAT, AND GIMME MONEY!!

RUSTLE

OKEY-DOKEY.

IN THAT CASE...

I SAID IT'S FINE! JUST SHUT UP AND DO IT!

REALLY SURE??

YEAH!!

I'LL DO IT, THEN, BUT... YOU'RE SURE?

HUP!

GJIGYAAAH!

GLUP GLUP

HUH ...?

...

TWITE!

TWITE!

WHAT'S GOING ON?!

?!

BARO !!

WAAAAARGH!

BLOO SO?!!

Gweh...

BLUP

BLORCH

HYEEGH...

...

HIS MAGIC IS SWELLING UP?!

BLORF BLORF BLORF

!!

WHAT IS THAT?!

GAJUICHI!

LET'S GO, MARIE.

WHAT!

MISTER GAUCHE!

HUH ...?!

I'LL TAKE YOU HOME THIS TIME FOR SURE, ASTA.

HEH HEH HEH!

✿ Page 44: Siblings

IN ANY CASE, WE HAVE TO GET THE CHILDREN AWAY!!

WE CAN'T HANDLE SOMETHING THAT BIG!

FLIP

BOOMF

BOOMF

BO OMF

WHAT'S GOING ON?!

Flame Creation Magic:

Guiding Light Leopard

FWOOSH

WE'LL NEED SOME TIME TO LET THEM ALL GET AWAY. UNTIL THEN, WE HAVE TO HOLD THIS POSITION!!

It's warm!

ALL RIGHT! RIDE ON THAT AND ESCAPE, A FEW AT A TIME!

GWoo+ ...

BLUCH

D... die...

...

Every... body...

Die...

BIG BROTHER BARO...!

DON'T YOU... KNOW ME?

WHAT... HAPPENED TO YOU?!

SKA

WHY...
DID YOU...

WHY SAVE
ME?!

BWOOOSH

HUH
...?

YOU HAVEN'T TAKEN ANY RESPONSIBILITY FOR THIS YET!!

UNTIL YOU DO, I'M NOT LETTING YOU DIE!!

IT LOOKS LIKE MY SWORD WORKS ON YOU, SO I'LL JUST KEEP RIGHT ON...

AND, HEY, DID YOU JUST TRY TO KILL YOUR LITTLE BROTHER?! HOW BIG OF AN IDIOT ARE YOU?!

...

THE DARK MAGIC ITEM I JUST INJECTED HIM WITH EATS THE SUBJECT'S LIFE ENERGY...

...AND PRODUCES AN EXPLOSION OF MAGIC POWER.

BOOSH

WHAT THE?!!

SKASSSH

ARRRRGH!

THERE'S NO END TO IT!!

IF HE'S LIKE THAT, EVEN WITH ANTI-MAGIC, YOU WON'T BE ABLE TO TAKE HIM DOWN EASILY.

GEH!

TAKE THAT!

YOU'RE WIDE OPEN, ASTA!

FINE WORDS, YOUNG WHIPPER-SNAPPER!

I'M NOT INTERESTED IN AN OLD LADY WHO USES WEAK, DRIED-UP MAGIC!

AWW! YOU GOT IN THE WAY AGAIN! QUIT BUTTING IN!

HOWEVER, THE POWER TO WORK WITH THE MANA THAT DWELLS IN NATURE CAN BE INCREASED AT ANY AGE.

TRUE, AS YOU AGE, THE MAGIC YOU CAN GENERATE INTERNALLY WEAKENS.

DON'T UNDER-ESTIMATE OLD HAGS!!

I HAVE YEARS OF EXPERIENCE COMBINED WITH TECHNIQUE. I WON'T LOSE TO A YOUNGSTER.

IF YOU KICK THE BUCKET, DON'T COME CRYING TO ME!

HMM... NOISY OLD LADY, AREN'T YOU!

CURSES... IF THIS GOES ON, THINGS WILL ONLY GET WORSE!!

THAT SAID, I CAN'T FIGHT PROPERLY IF I'M PROTECTING THE CHILDREN AND HELPING THEM ESCAPE AT THE SAME TIME!

GAUCHE...! WHY DID THAT IDIOT RUN AWAY?!

BUT THE OTHERS...! PLEASE GO BACK!

GAUCHE, GO BACK!!

NOPE.

NO. I'M TAKING YOU BACK TO TOWN, MARIE.

AS LONG AS YOU'RE OKAY, MARIE, I DON'T CARE ABOUT ANYBODY ELSE.

IF I FOUGHT THAT, I'D BE PUTTING YOU IN DANGER.

MY MAGIC DOESN'T WORK ON THAT WOMAN, AND NOW THERE'S AN INSANELY POWERFUL MONSTER TOO.

I CAN'T STAND SEEING YOU THIS UNCOOL, GAUCHE!

I HATE IT!!!

BUT SISTER THERESA AND THE CHILDREN FROM THE CHURCH ARE DIFFERENT! THEY'RE ALL GOOD PEOPLE!!

YOU'RE RIGHT. LOTS OF PEOPLE DID LOTS OF MEAN THINGS TO US...

WE'RE WHO WE ARE... BECAUSE THEY'RE HERE!!

EVERYONE'S LIVES ARE CONNECTED, YOU KNOW?!

Heeeeey!

OH!

MARCO!

HWOOO

GAUCHE, PLEASE GO SAVE EVERYBODY!

I'LL WAIT HERE WITH MARCO, SO...

THAT'S JUST LIKE THEM!

SISTER THERESA AND ASTA SAVED ME.

MARCO, YOU'RE OKAY! I'M SO GLAD!

You better believe you will, you little punk. If anything happens to Marie, I'll kick your little...

GAUCHE!

THOOM THOOM

GRIT GRIT

GRA

I'LL PROTECT MARIE. YOU CAN COUNT ON ME!

ASTA LOANED IT TO ME. HE SAID IT WOULD MAKE ME BRAVE!

HEY, KID. THAT ROBE...

THE CAPTAIN AND THE OTHER BRIGADE MEMBERS THINK HE'S REALLY SOMETHING, BUT THAT WOMAN CAUGHT HIM IN NO TIME.

"ASTA, ASTA, ASTA." EVERYBODY AND THEIR COUSIN... WHAT'S SO GREAT ABOUT THAT GUY, ANYWAY?

WHEN YOU GET RIGHT DOWN TO IT, EVERYBODY VALUES THEMSELVES OVER OTHER PEOPLE.

AND ANYWAY, I BET HE AND THE HAG BOTH GAVE UP AND RAN OFF.

QUIT PROTECT-ING...?

I'M A MAGIC KNIGHT.

GEEZ, YOU'RE STUBBORN.

QUIT PROTECTING THOSE GUYS AND LET ME CATCH YOU, ASTA.

TO BE CONTINUED IN VOLUME 6!

The Blank Page Brigade

This volume's topic: Unlucky things that happened to you recently.

The toilet clogged.
Asahi Sakano

I broke my smartphone on New Year's Day.
Genya Hori

I went out on a day when lots of snow had fallen, and my shoes got soaking wet...
Hayato Goto

I lost weight once, but I got fat again.
Masayoshi Satoshō

My eyes are squinty.
Koki Ishikawa

A pigeon pooped on a book I'd borrowed from my friend. ...Right in front of the friend.
Ko Shimameguri

I forget stuff so often it's not even funny.
Teruaki Mizuno

THE FINAL

My daughter (ten months) gives me fake smiles...
Comics Editor Tomiyama

ULTRA SOOOOUL!!!

During a meeting, Tabata Sensei was so tired he fell asleep.
Editor Katayama

I got drunk and lost my shoes. (for the second time)
Designer Iwai

Nothing in particular.
©

AAAH!!
ROLL
ROLL
Wife's hand

In one year, I've gained a whole 10 kg.
Captain Tabata

AFTERWORD

❋

This time, guess what?!
I got a comment from Honoka Akimoto, one of the members of the very happening idol singer group Team Shachihoko! (It's on Page 154.)
Thank you very much!

I also got a signed DVD and CD, and I'm letting the fantastic performances and singing boost my morale.

I couldn't be happier or more grateful that a person like that, someone who can cheer people up, is reading my manga! I'll keep doing my very best! Raaaaaaah!!

Special Bonus Materials

Presenting early sketches of the Eye of the Midnight Sun members! And was there a phantom fourth girl at that mixer?!

Sally

Rades

The girls from
the mixer chapter.

Baro

Neige

DEMON SLAYER

KIMETSU NO YAIBA

Story and Art by
KOYOHARU GOTOUGE

In Taisho-era Japan, kindhearted Tanjiro Kamado makes a living selling charcoal. But his peaceful life is shattered when a demon slaughters his entire family. His little sister Nezuko is the only survivor, but she has been transformed into a demon herself! Tanjiro sets out on a dangerous journey to find a way to return his sister to normal and destroy the demon who ruined his life.

VIZ

NARUTO

Story and Art by
Masashi Kishimoto

Naruto is determined to become the greatest ninja ever!

Twelve years ago the Village Hidden
in the Leaves was attacked by a
fearsome threat. A nine-tailed fox
spirit claimed the life of the village
leader, the Hokage, and many others.
Today, the village is at peace and a
troublemaking kid named Naruto is
struggling to graduate from Ninja
Academy. His goal may be to become
the next Hokage, but his true destiny
will be much more complicated.
The adventure begins now!

WORLD'S BEST SELLING MANGA!

www.shonenjump.com   www.viz.com

Stop

YOU'RE READING
THE WRONG WAY!

BLACK CLOVER

reads from right to left, starting
in the upper-right corner. Japanese
is read from right to left, meaning
that action, sound effects, and
word-balloon order are completely
reversed from English order.